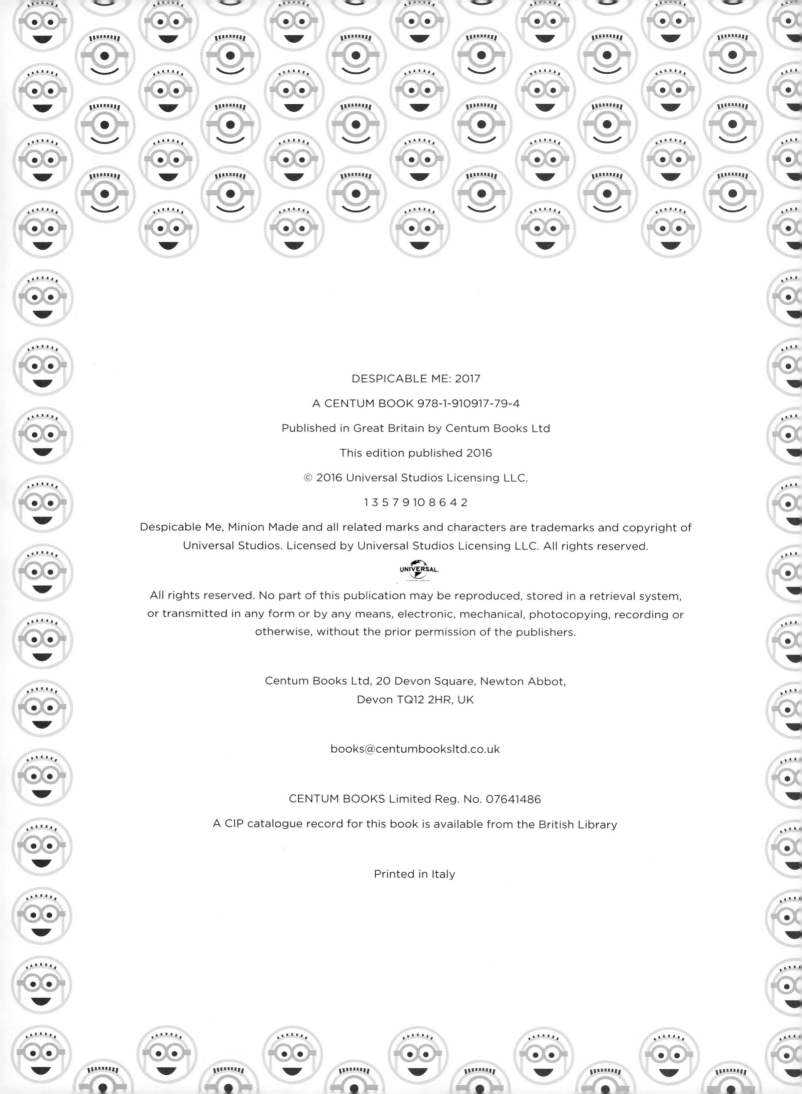

DESPICABLE ME: 2017

A CENTUM BOOK 978-1-910917-79-4

Published in Great Britain by Centum Books Ltd

This edition published 2016

© 2016 Universal Studios Licensing LLC.

1 3 5 7 9 10 8 6 4 2

Centum Books Ltd, 20 Devon Square, Newton Abbot,
Devon TQ12 2HR, UK

books@centumbooksltd.co.uk

CENTUM BOOKS Limited Reg. No. 07641486

A CIP catalogue record for this book is available from the British Library

Printed in Italy

DESPICABLE ME

MINION MADE ™

2017

THIS MINION-TASTIC BOOK BELONGS TO:

centum

WHAT'S INSIDE?

7	Join the Tribe!
8	What's your Minion-ish name?
9	Minion Me!
10	Bello Minions!
12	Silly Search
13	Which Minion is your buddy?
14	Minion Story: Part 1
22	How Yellow Are You?
23	Feeling Griddy
24	Let's Boogie!
25	Minion Master
26	Goggle-eyed Gadget
28	Secret Shadows
29	Disguise this Minion
30	Master Matches
31	Bob's Buddy
32	Millions of Minions
34	True or False
35	Speedy Tricks
36	Minion Story: Part 2
44	Could you be a Minion Master?
46	Master of Masters
47	Time to Find a New Master
48	What Are They Thinking?
50	Me Take a Selfie!
51	In a Spin
52	A Little Odd
53	Feeding Time!
54	Minion Games
56	Mastermind Quiz
60	Answers

JOIN THE TRIBE!

Are you feeling particularly yellow today? Join the gang of mischievous Minions on a journey of Gru-some games and despicable puzzles.

- Do your henchman duties and beat the word games
- Assist the evil masters and spot the differences
- Go a bit wild on the colouring pages
- ... and prepare to get through a LOT of bananas

MINIONS ASSEMBLE!

LOOK OUT FOR THESE GOGGLE LETTERS THROUGHOUT THE BOOK. FIND 10 LETTERS THEN UNSCRAMBLE THEM HERE TO WORK OUT THE MYSTERY WORD.

— — — — — — — — — —

WHAT'S YOUR MINION-ISH NAME?

For such strange-looking little guys, the Minions have oddly normal names.

Which Minion name would suit you? Pick your favourite picture in the top row and your favourite picture in the left column, then see where they meet in the grid!

KEVIN	LARRY	JERRY	TONY	CHRIS
CARL	STUART	BOB	PHIL	KEVIN
TIM	MARK	JORGE	HENRY	TOM
BOB	DAVE	JON	CARL	KEN
 JOHN	JOSH	LANCE	NORBERT	STUART

MINION ME!

So, one eye or two? Combed hair or wild spikes? Turn yourself into a Minion!

Draw your outfit, fill in your profile, then sign your new Minion name on your badge.

HELLO
MY MINION NAME IS

Favourite Minion word:

_____

Best yellow possession:

_____

Number of bananas I eat in a day:

_____

Favourite Minion master:

_____

Minion best buddy:

_____

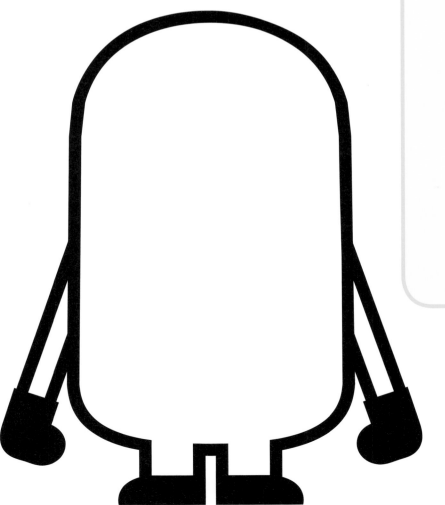

BELLO MINIONS!

The loveable guys may look similar, but they're just as different as humans! Meet some of your favourite Minions and see what sets them apart.

DAVE is pretty clever – for a Minion! But he's not very patient. When Gru was about to share his latest despicable plot, Dave got over-excited and fired his rocket launcher into a bunch of Minions! Oops.

LOVES: video games, ice cream, rocket launchers.

Musician. Lover. Hungry. These are three words that describe **STUART**. He didn't realise that he was born for adventure until he took a nap and was volunteered to join Kevin on his mission to find a new boss.

LOVES: playing his ukulele, hot tubs and food.

BOB is the smallest Minion. However, what he lacks in size he makes up for in heart. He loves adventures, exploring and making new friends . . . actually he loves everything – that's what makes him so loveable.

LOVES: his teddy bear Tim, giggling, playing hide-and-seek, making friends.

If you're in need of a plan or a Minion of action – **KEVIN** is the one you want. He's the one with a plan to find the tribe a new evil boss to serve.

LOVES: Protecting his buddies, epic adventures, heists, awesome gadgets.

Short and plump, **PHIL** is the ultimate Minion giggler and will laugh at just about anything. In his spare time, he enjoys cleaning in a French maid's outfit.

LOVES: Karaoke, dressing up, kisses from Agnes.

Small in size, but big on fun, you'll sometimes hear **CARL** shouting 'Bee-do, bee-do'. Why? Because he's being a fire siren, of course. He's very handy with a fire extinguisher.

LOVES: Skateboarding, making noises.

Draw the Minion-you waving 'Bello'!

SILLY SEARCH

Don't be bored silly! Test your goggles and find the Minion-related words in the monstrously-big wordsearch.

H	N	S	G	I	G	G	L	E	H	G	N	F	A	P	F
N	T	A	U	P	Y	O	H	D	O	L	D	E	G	N	V
G	H	O	I	S	O	G	M	G	R	E	N	I	G	S	N
Y	N	P	T	O	N	G	N	R	K	H	O	H	L	O	H
O	S	B	A	P	P	L	E	K	H	S	Y	C	E	P	N
Y	A	P	R	D	N	E	P	H	O	N	S	S	H	A	P
S	U	G	S	I	Y	S	P	O	R	Y	E	I	T	N	D
M	A	S	T	E	R	O	D	R	K	K	K	M	N	H	R
A	O	B	E	T	A	K	H	W	H	O	O	N	O	R	A
D	T	O	N	P	B	A	N	A	N	A	A	D	V	K	O
Y	A	A	K	H	U	H	A	H	S	G	R	Y	E	H	B
E	S	B	A	N	A	N	S	B	G	A	A	P	R	O	E
L	H	O	Y	S	D	A	N	C	E	K	K	R	A	R	T
L	O	T	P	N	N	A	T	O	D	T	Y	N	L	H	A
O	A	P	Y	A	O	P	D	H	S	N	O	T	L	E	K
W	E	S	I	U	G	S	I	D	O	T	A	P	S	P	S

YELLOW
OVERALLS
GOGGLES
BANANA
BAPPLE
DISGUISE
MISCHIEF

DANCE
GUITAR
SKATEBOARD
KARAOKE
GIGGLE
MASTER

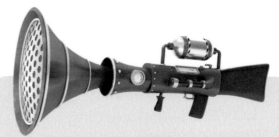

UNSCRAMBLE the highlighted letters to reveal one of the Minions' favourite gross gadgets:

_ _ _ _ _ _ _ _

ANSWERS ON page 60

WHICH MINION IS YOUR BUDDY?

Which yellow dude would be your partner in crime?

Answer the questions and follow the arrows to find out.

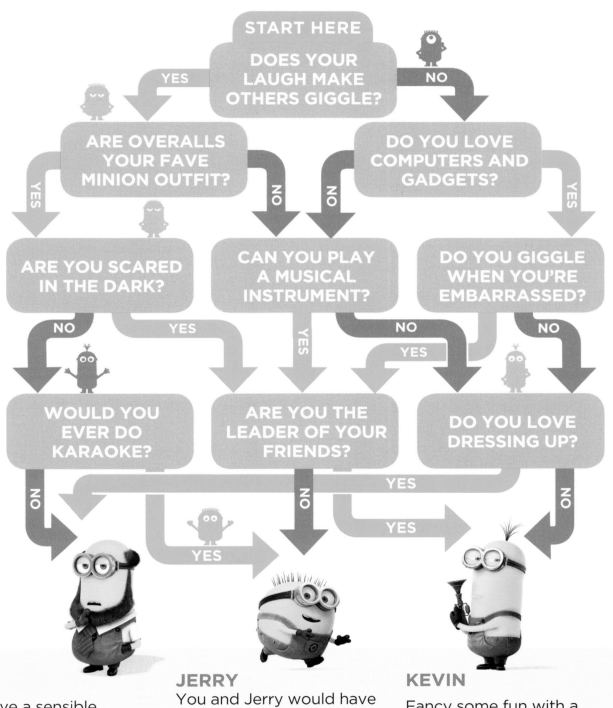

START HERE

DOES YOUR LAUGH MAKE OTHERS GIGGLE?

YES → **ARE OVERALLS YOUR FAVE MINION OUTFIT?**

NO → **DO YOU LOVE COMPUTERS AND GADGETS?**

YES → **ARE YOU SCARED IN THE DARK?**

NO → **CAN YOU PLAY A MUSICAL INSTRUMENT?**

NO

YES → **DO YOU GIGGLE WHEN YOU'RE EMBARRASSED?**

NO → **WOULD YOU EVER DO KARAOKE?**

YES → **ARE YOU THE LEADER OF YOUR FRIENDS?**

NO / YES

NO → **DO YOU LOVE DRESSING UP?**

YES

YES

YES

NO

NO

TIM
You have a sensible side, but you're also a master of mischief (and a fan of massage chairs). The perfect pal for Tim!

JERRY
You and Jerry would have endless giggles, then you could sing Minionese while he plays the guitar.

KEVIN
Fancy some fun with a Fart Gun? Then Kev's your best buddy. Have a giggle discovering the best Minion weapons and gadgets.

MINIONS:
STORY OF THE MOVIE

Minions have been on Earth since the beginning of time. They want just one thing: to find the biggest, baddest master to serve.

Keeping a master wasn't easy – at first each master was eventually replaced – or eaten – by a bigger, badder boss.

When they finally left the sea, the Minions found the giant T. rex. It was love at first sight . . . until they accidently knocked the T. rex into a volcano!

Whoops!

During the Stone Age mankind emerged. The Minions took an instant liking to man and wanted to serve him well. When a bear came after him, they handed the man a flyswatter to fend off the bear.

It seemed like a good idea – it wasn't. The bear won the fight.

Next, the Minions found a pharaoh in ancient Egypt who asked the Minions to build his pyramid. But the Minions built it upside down; it fell over, squashing their master flat.

But Minions do not give up.

They found another master in the Dark Ages – Dracula.

Who knew if they opened the curtains the sunlight would turn him to ash?!

The Minions nearly killed Napoleon with a poorly aimed cannon blast. His army pursued the Minions for hundreds of miles.

They finally found refuge in a cave. Here they forged their own civilisation.

At first it was fun. But with no leader to serve, the Minions had no purpose.

But all was not lost. For one Minion had hope.

His name . . .

. . . was Kevin.

Kevin revealed his big plan to his buddies. He would leave the cave and find the biggest, baddest master for the Minions to serve. But he needed help.

"Me coming!" Bob yelled.

Kevin looked down at Bob; he was the smallest Minion and Kevin worried that Bob was not strong enough for the dangerous journey ahead.

Thankfully a Minion in the back raised a ukulele in the air. It was a sleepy one-eyed Minion named Stuart, whose friends were playing a trick on him.

Stuart stood up, and joined Kevin, not really sure why everyone was clapping for him.

Bob was Kevin's only other option.

"Ugh . . ." Kevin huffed. "Komay."

Bob grabbed his teddy bear Tim and was ready to go.

MINIONS:
STORY OF THE MOVIE

"Big boss! Big boss!" chanted the tribe as Kevin, Stuart and Bob walked towards the cave exit and off to find their new boss!

The journey was treacherous. They hiked over mountains, through the dense forests and paddled across an ocean in a canoe.

They slept. They got hungry, and food was scarce. Stuart became so hungry he imaged Bob and Kevin were bananas and started licking them! But then they saw a beautiful woman in the distance. And she was . . . green?!

It was the Statue of Liberty. Kevin, Stuart and Bob had reached New York City in all its 1960s glory.

First things first, they needed new clothes and Kevin spotted something perfect, denim and blue . . .

"*Bueno!*" Stuart said, turning round so he could see his reflection in the glass window. His bum looked good . . . really good.

Then they took off through the streets, dwarfed by the giant buildings, hot-dog stands and even the fire hydrants . . . by everything, really.

Bob got distracted by a woman in a banana-print dress and followed her into a taxi. Stuart and Kevin searched for their lost friend. Finally they spotted him going into a department store and followed him. Suddenly the lights went out. The Minions wandered around to find that the store was closed. They'd be stuck inside for the night.

Kevin found a big bed with a TV in front of it. They huddled together and switched on the TV.

Stuart wiggled the antennae, until suddenly a man in a black suit appeared on the screen. "You're watching the top-secret Villain Network Channel," he said. "If you tell anyone, we'll find you."

There were pictures of a giant convention with different villains.

"VNC is sponsored by Villain-Con. For eighty-nine years the biggest gathering of criminals anywhere," the man said. "Plus a special appearance from the first female super villain . . . Scarlet Overkill!"

A woman's silhouette appeared on screen. Even her shadow seemed menacing.

This was it . . . the master they'd been looking for.

"Get to Villain-Con this weekend. Only at 545 Orange Grove Avenue in Orlando, Florida," the announcer said.

Kevin stood up, jumping on the bed. "Villain-Con! Orlando! La big boss!"

B

Kevin, Stuart, and Bob needed a ride to Orlando, wherever that was. As they walked along a highway, leaving the city, Kevin picked up a piece of cardboard and wrote *Orlando* on it. It wasn't long before a car came towards him and screeched to a stop.

"All aboard the Nelson Express!" the man inside bellowed. The Minions scrambled inside and were on their way to Villain-Con with the Nelson's, a loving family of criminals.

After hours of driving, "we're here," yelled Walter, "Villain-Con!"

The Minions looked out of the window. The car was moving into an underground convention hall.

"Villain-Con!" Stuart cried. "La Villain-Con!"

All around was a sea of villains of all shapes and sizes.

Kevin pulled Stuart and Bob towards the hall. This was the moment they'd been waiting for. Scarlet's voice boomed, "Doesn't it feel so good to be bad?" Then, she burst through the screen and used her jetpack dress to rocket around the hall.

"Have any of you ever dreamed of working for the greatest super villain of all time? Well, what if I told you that I am looking for new henchmen?"

The Minions felt like they were going to explode. Kevin rubbed his ears. Did she just say she needed new henchmen?!

"It's just a matter of proving you're good enough," Scarlet went on. "Just take this ruby from my hand and you've got the job . . ."

Hundreds of villains rushed towards Scarlet. She whirled round and sent them flying backwards off the stage.

Kevin looked at the pile of defeated henchmen. The Minions wanted to serve the biggest, baddest boss, but they wanted to leave intact!

Just then, Bob's teddy bear Tim slipped from his hands and was kicked across the stage and Kevin saw the ruby thrown high in the air.

When Scarlet had fought off the last of the villains, she looked around.

"Didn't my speech inspire anyone?" she yelled. "All these villains and I still have the . . ." Scarlet realised that she didn't have the ruby. Instead she was holding Bob's teddy bear. "Who has the ruby?" she shrieked.

Bob coughed and spat the ruby onto the floor.

Scarlet smiled. "The job has been filled!" She whisked Kevin, Stuart and Bob into her sleek, futuristic red jet, and they set off.

minions:
STORY OF THE MOVIE

Scarlet's jet travelled so fast it wasn't long before they reached England and her castle in the middle of London. "Herb! My baby!" Scarlet called inside. She hugged her husband, a sleek inventor named Herb.

"Herb, these are the new recruits: Kevin, Stuart and Bob," Scarlet said.

"Right on." Herb laughed. "You guys are crazy little and way yellow and I dig that!"

Scarlet looked seriously at the Minions. "Okay, listen up! It's time to get down to business." She pointed to a painting. "This is Queen Elizabeth," Scarlet said, "Ruler of England, and I really, really want her crown. Steal me the crown and all your dreams come true. But if you fail, I'll blow you off the face of the Earth. OK?"

Kevin, Stuart and Bob went to Herb's lab. They needed gadgets to help them. In the lab the Minions saw a large metal machine.

"When it's finished it'll be my Ultimate Weapon," Herb told them. "So, you're here for gear . . ."

The Minions nodded.

Herb looked down at Bob. "You get my Far-out Stretch Suit."

"Kevin," Herb went on. "You are the proud owner of this lava gun."

"And finally, Stu," Herb said. "Behold the Hypno-Hat!"

The next morning the Minions went to the Tower of London to steal the queen's crown. They sneaked inside as a group of guards approached.

Stuart pushed the button on the side of his Hypno-Hat. The guards were hypnotised and started to dance around. The Minions ran past the guards and towards the back entrance of the Crown Jewels room.

Kevin pulled out his Lava-Lamp Gun, fired a blast and melted a hole right through the steel. There was the queen's crown. The Minions ran as the display case lowered into the floor.

The crown was taken by the queen's guards into a horse-drawn carriage. The Minions ran to catch it up.

Bob activated his Stretch Suit. He made his legs two stories high, grabbed his friends, and ran after the carriage. He flung Kevin and Stuart inside the Queen's carriage.

"Gimme la crowna!" Stuart yelled at the queen. Hundreds of police chased after the carriage. "After them!" the queen shouted.

Bob ran all the way to a square and grabbed a sword that was wedged into a giant boulder. The crowd fell silent. The clouds above parted, casting Bob in a heavenly glow.

It had long been said that no one except a true king could pull the sword from the stone. But now Bob had done it. He was the new king of England!

HOW YELLOW ARE YOU?

Have you been hanging out with the yellow guys for too long?

Tick all the statements that you agree with, then find out just how goggly-eyed you are!

I like bananas ☐

The T. rex is my fave dino ☐

If music comes on, I HAVE to dance ☐

I can play the guitar ☐

I have lots of buddies ☐

I sometimes say 'Bello' instead of 'Hello' ☐

I make the perfect assistant ☐

Cupcakes are awesome ☐

Every day should be fancy dress ☐

Skateboarding is Minion-tastic ☐

I once made a birthday cake for a vampire ☐

I sometimes wear overalls ☐

I'd love to own a Fart Gun ☐

Bottom jokes make me laugh ☐

Goggles are an excellent fashion accessory! ☐

HOW MANY BOXES DID YOU TICK?

YOU ARE THIS MUCH MINION!

10 to 15 COLOUR to here

5 to 10 COLOUR to here

0 to 5 COLOUR to here

FEELING GRIDDY

Get that mastermind ticking over and write the correct name next to each Minion.

Then take it to evil genius level, and fit all the names into the grid.

a

_ _ _

b

_ _ M

c

_ _ _ L

d

_ _ _

e

_ _ R _ _

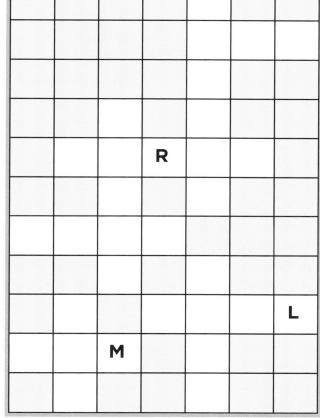

i

_ _ _ _ _

f

_ _ _ _ _ _ _

g

_ _ _ _ _ _

h

_ _ _ _ _

ANSWERS ON
page 60

LET'S BOOGIE!

If there's a beat then you can be sure that the Minions can't resisit dancing to it!

Can you work out which guy comes next in each sequence?
Circle your answer.

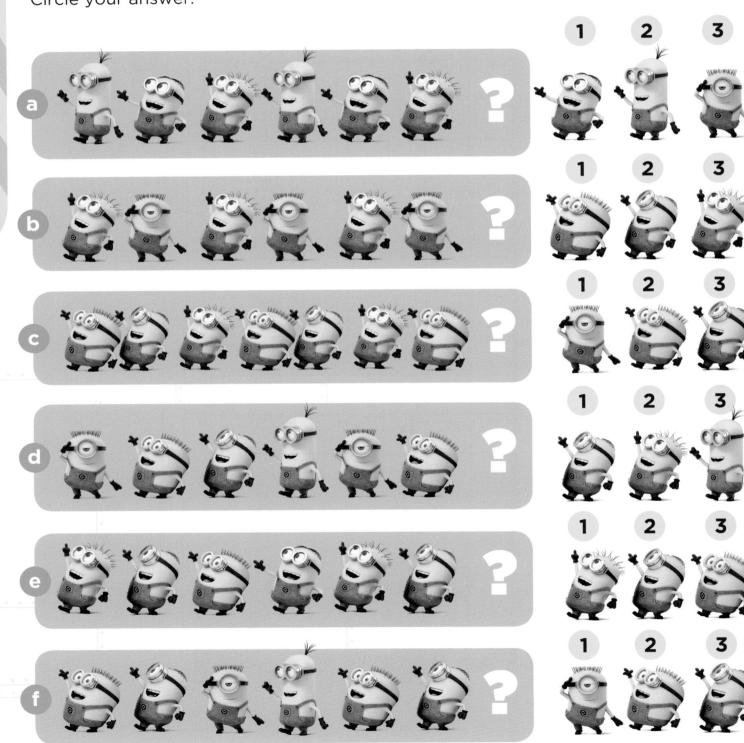

ANSWERS ON
page 60

Minions without a master are Minions without a purpose.

Help them design a Wanted poster to find the villainous leader of their dreams!

MASTER WANTED

- GOOD AT BEING BAD.
- PLENTY OF NEFARIOUS SCHEMES UP THEIR SLEEVE.
- A NEED FOR HUNDREDS OF HENCHMEN.

My amazing Minion master is called: _____

GOGGLE-EYED GADGET

The Minions may not seem like the smartest bunch, but they're a whizz with computers and gadgets.

Use the space to test some designs, then create a new gadget for your favourite Minion.

What is it called?

_____

What does it do?

_____

What are its special features?

_____

Why does it make you giggle?

_____

SECRET SHADOWS

Another day, another dodgy disguise!
These guys never turn down an opportunity to dress up.

Can you match the madcap Minions to their shadows?

ANSWERS ON
page 60

DISGUISE THIS MINION

Now it's your turn for some dress-up design!

This Minion is going undercover on a secret, master-criminal plot to a celebrity awards ceremony. How will you disguise him so he doesn't get spotted?

MASTER MATCHES

The Minions like to show dedication to their masters – that's why they co-ordinate fashion with their bosses!

Draw a line to match each Minion to the master you think he was serving – according to his outfit.

a

b

c

d

e

1 The Minions got to a bit of a rocky start with **T. rex,** and things heated up when they accidentally caused him to fall into a lava pit.

2 The **caveman** was in trouble when the Minions got him too close to a bear. That master only lasted through one more meal – he was the dinner.

3 Ancient Egypt seemed like the perfect place to use their building skills. The **Pharoah** agreed – until he was squashed by their first pyramid.

4 **Dracula** was quite an easy master. He always slept through the day. Remember when the Minions woke him up on his birthday in the daylight? It was Dracula's last birthday.

5 Le Minions served **Napoleon** with great pride. It was going so well, too, until they shot him with a cannonball and were chased away.

ANSWERS ON page 60

Bob's got a mission for you – it's top secret and more important than a royal jewel heist, or even a whole bunch of bananas.

Join the dots to reunite Bob with his best buddy.

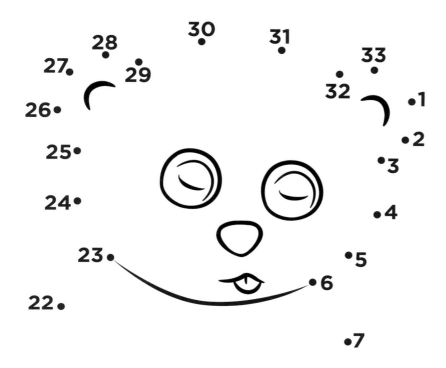

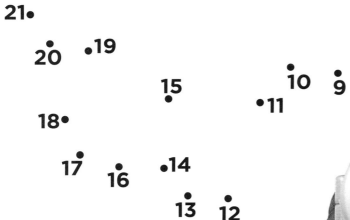

MILLIONS OF MINIONS

Do you know what you can't have enough of – Minions
How many can you count on these pages?

33

TRUE OR FALSE

Totally true or complete con?

Avoid the villainous fibs about the Minions, and circle the true statements.

1 Minions have four fingers on each hand.   T or F

2 Minions can breathe in outer space.   T or F

3 One-eyed Minions are always bigger than their two-eyed friends.   T or F

4 Minions have five different natural hairstyles.   T or F

5 The 'Minion' word for Goodbye is Poopaye.   T or F

6 Minions are very easily distracted.   T or F

7 Minions enjoy making photocopies of their bottom.   T or F

8 Minions only eat bananas.   T or F

9 Minions can't dance.   T or F

Uh-oh, Jerry's behind the wheel of Lucy's car!

Can you spot eight differences between the pictures before the little guy spins out of control?

COLOUR a mini car for every difference you spot.

1

2

ANSWERS ON
page 60

A reporter stood outside Buckingham Palace. "One of England's most famous myths has become a reality," he said, talking into a camera. "Bob has pulled the famed sword right from its stone and is the new king."

Scarlet was watching the news. "Tiny yellow traitors!" she shouted at the TV.

At the palace, a line of guards, on Bob's request, were all wearing yellow outfits and goggles.

"Awwwww buddies!" Bob yelled. He'd only been at the palace for a few minutes, but it already felt like home.

The Minions were playing in the great hall. Kevin hit a polo ball across the room. Just then, the door swung open. The ball smacked Scarlet Overkill right on the nose.

"How dare you!" she yelled, her face red.

"You little traitors!" she fumed. "You stole my dream! I was going to be made queen and you pinheads screwed it up!"

Kevin plucked the crown from Bob's head and gave it to Scarlet, trying to make amends.

The Minions took everyone into the Houses of Parliament, where Bob as king declared Scarlet as the new queen of England. "La keena pota Scarlet po papiel!" Bob shouted.

Scarlet turned to the Minions. "Come with me," she said. "You're finally going to get everything you deserve."

The Minions skipped through the palace. This was it – finally their master would reward them for all their hard work. Scarlet led them to some stairs at the far end of the palace. Kevin, Stuart and Bob had only taken a few steps, when Scarlet slammed the door behind them. Slowly their eyes adjusted to the dark. Metal torture devices covered the walls. She'd locked them in the palace dungeon . . .

They crawled out of the sewer next to where Scarlet was being crowned. The doors were locked. They would have to climb inside the cathedral.

Inside the cathedral the Minions saw Scarlet standing below them.

Suddenly a bee started circling Bob's head. Stuart and Bob were forced on to the chandelier. The bee chased the Minions in circles. Stuart and Bob kept running, trying to get away from it, but the more they ran, the more unsteady the chandelier became. The screw that held it to the roof came loose.

Far below, Scarlet smiled as the archbishop stepped forward with the crown. "I proclaim thee, with great reservation, the queen of England!"

Hearing the commotion, Scarlet looked up just as the chandelier fell from the ceiling. Kevin managed to grab Stuart and Bob before it plummeted to the ground and landed on top of Scarlet.

The Minions hadn't meant to hurt Scarlet, but they knew that this did not look good!

Suddenly they heard a crash. Scarlet shot up towards the ceiling. She had been protected by her dress – a new state-of-the-art villain suit that Herb had designed. She hovered, staring at the Minions, her face red with rage.

She pointed at the Minions. "Get them!" she shouted to the crowd.

The Minions ran, trying to lose the angry villains. But villains emerged from everywhere. Kevin got separated from his friends. He kept glancing back, but he couldn't see them anywhere.

Kevin kept running, until he saw a television set. A reporter was speaking into the camera, until Scarlet pushed him out of the way.

"Kevin, I know you're out there!" she screeched into the camera. "Look what we have here!"

She reached down, pulling up Stuart and Bob. They were both tied up.

"Buddies!" cried Kevin.

He had to help his friends!

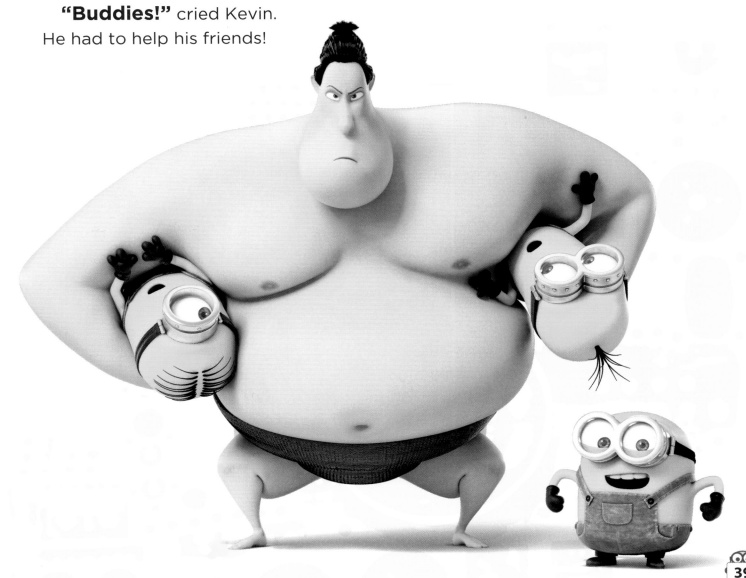

Kevin broke inside Herb's lab; he needed supplies! He tumbled into Herb's Ultimate Weapon and activated it. "Three . . . two . . . one . . ." said a mechanical voice. The machine started to work. Kevin grew . . . and grew . . . until he was thirty stories tall.

"Buddies!"

he cried and he stomped off to find them.

Stuart and Bob sat tied to sticks of dynamite. "This is it, boys," said Scarlet.

They struggled against the rope, watching in panic as the fuse burned lower and lower . . .

Wham!

A giant boot slammed down on the fuse, snuffing it out.

"Bello!" Giant Kevin cried out.

Kevin tried to free his friends, but someone was behind him. "So that's your plan?" Scarlet shouted as she flew behind him. "Make yourself a bigger target?"

Luckily, Kevin had called the tribe earlier to tell them he'd found a new boss and to come to London. So when he looked at the other side of the street and saw a huge crowd – he saw his buddies! Not just Stuart and Bob, but all of them. They were ready to fight with him.

"This ends now!" Scarlet growled.

Scarlet's dress activated into its final stage, revealing a nuclear core. She aimed the bomb at the Minions and fired. Kevin took a step forward, leaned in . . . and swallowed it.

"Have fun exploding!" Scarlet cackled.

Scarlet scooped up Herb and flew off. She wanted to get as far away as possible. Kevin grabbed them and was dragged along. The beeping inside Kevin sped up. The bomb was about to go off. "No, no, no, no, no!" Scarlet cried.

Booooooooooooom!

MINIONS:
STORY OF THE MOVIE

The Minions watched in horror as the sky was filled with smoke. It took them a moment to notice the speck of yellow in the sky.

"Looka!" Bob cried, showing the other Minions. It was Kevin floating back down to earth, using his blue overalls as a parachute and he was back to his normal size.

The Minions had done it – they had saved all of London from Scarlet Overkill, the tyrant queen. But Scarlet's story wasn't over quite yet . . .

Scarlet and Herb hurtled through the sky until they crashed in the middle of a snowy wasteland.

"Where are we?" Scarlet said.

She looked up and saw several angry-looking Yetis. Scarlet wasn't intimidated. Within hours, she became their queen. It was the coronation she always wanted.

Life works in mysterious ways. Scarlet and Herb finally had a kingdom to rule. It didn't have a castle, but it was air-conditioned.

In London, Queen Elizabeth addressed a giant crowd.
"We are here today to celebrate the Minions.
The country owes you a great debt of gratitude."

"Kevin!" the queen said.
"You are a hero of the highest order.
For your bravery and valour, I am
knighting you. From here on out,
you are Sir Kevin. Well done."

The queen also thanked Bob by
giving him a tiny crown for his teddy,
Tim, and Stuart by giving him an
awesome electric guitar.

"Kevin! Kevin! Kevin!"
all the Minions chanted. They carried
their leader on their shoulders, into
the streets of London. Kevin had
saved the day and won the love
and respect of his tribe.

COULD YOU BE A MINION MASTER?

Remember Scarlet Overkill?

Think you've got what it takes to take over the world? Try this quiz to find out how supervillain you are.

1 What groovy gadget would you have?

2   Hypno-hat

3   Lava gun

1   Stretch suit

2 Who would be your supervillain buddy?

3   Scarlet Overkill

1   Mr Nelson

2   Broadsword

3 What would be your first villainous plan?

1   To rob a bank

2   To freeze ray other bad guys

3   To steal the moon

4 What would you do at Villain Con?

3   The keynote speech, like Scarlet

2   Present your latest evil gadget

1   Recruit new henchmen

5 Which bad guy would you award with 'bad-guy-of-the-month'?

1   Frankie Fishlips

3   Dumo

2   Sick Rick

6 What would be your best bad-guy talent?

2   Inventing evil gadgets

3   Coming up with evil plans

1   Finding the best evil henchmen

7 What's the most awesome heist?

1   Stealing teddy Tim from Bob

2   Stealing the Queen's crown

3   Pinching Scarlet's jet

8 What gives you the shivers?

1   Scarlet Overkill's bedtime stories

2   Frankie Fishlips' scaly skin

3   Dumo's thunderous footsteps

9 Which Nelson would you be?

2   Tina

3   Walter Junior

1   Baby Nelson

10 Could you pull off the crime of the century?

3   No problem

2   Maybe, with the right helpers

1   I'm probably too nice

RESULTS

VILLAIN-IN-TRAINING

Mostly **1**

Your problem is you're far too . . . good! Maybe a life of crime just isn't for you. You'll need a few lessons from Scarlet before you're ready for your own Minion helpers.

PRETTY DESPICABLE

Mostly **2**

You've got some supervillain skills, but you'll need more practice before you're ready for an army of henchmen. Think bigger and badder and you'll soon get there!

STAR SUPERVILLAIN

Mostly **3**

Does it feel good to be bad?! You could give Scarlet Overkill a run for her money. The Minions would go all googly-eyes as soon as they saw you . . . their new master!

Which Minion master do you think is the best villain ever?

Draw your favourite despicable boss and fill in their evil scorecard.

EVIL SCORECARD

NAME: _____

VILLANOUS LOOK:

WEAPONS:

CRIMINAL PLOTTING:

HENCHMEN:

OVERALL VILLAIN RATING:

TIME TO FIND A NEW MASTER

It's tricky to find the perfect master.

Can you find all these images in the big picture?

ANSWERS ON page 60

47

WHAT ARE THEY THINKING?

What goes through the minds of the mischievous Minions? Bananas? Their next gadget? Saving their master from his latest nefarious scheme? Bananas?

Fill the bubbles with pictures of their thoughts.

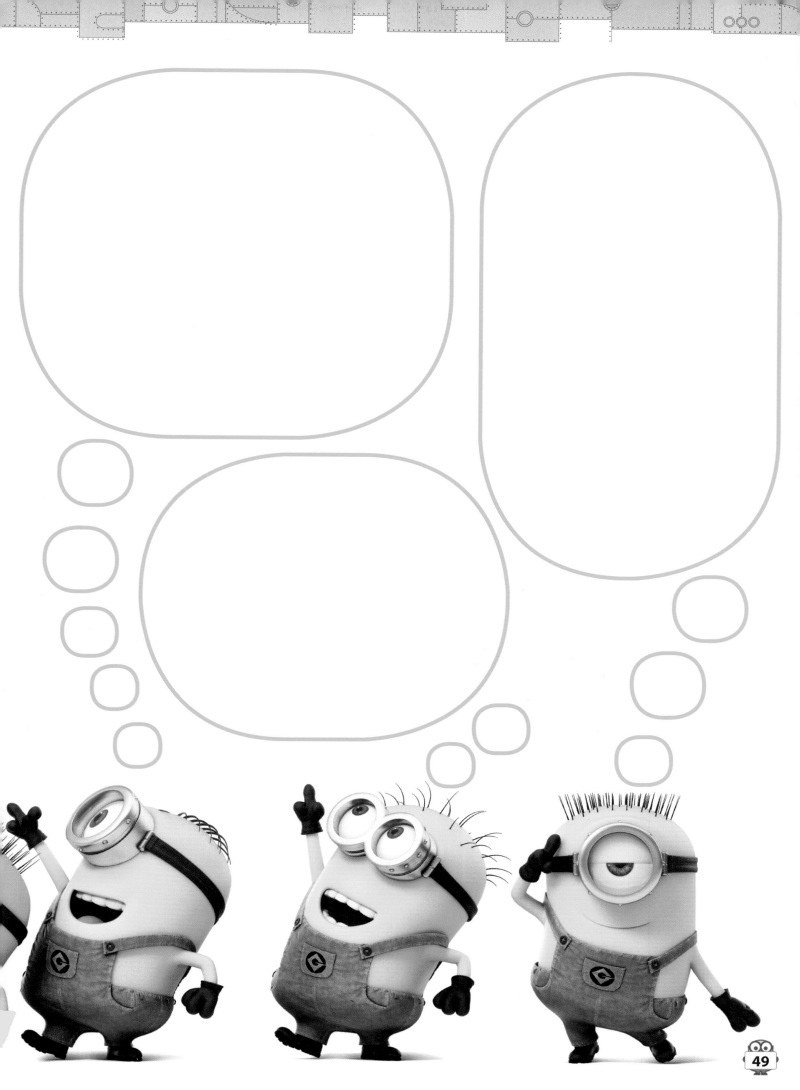

ME TAKE A SELFIE!

The Minions are trying to master the art of the perfect selfie. Unfortunately, they've messed it up!

Can you guess which character is in each close-up?

IN A SPIN

Can you solve this mind-boggling puzzle?

Start in the centre and answer the clues to complete the spiral.

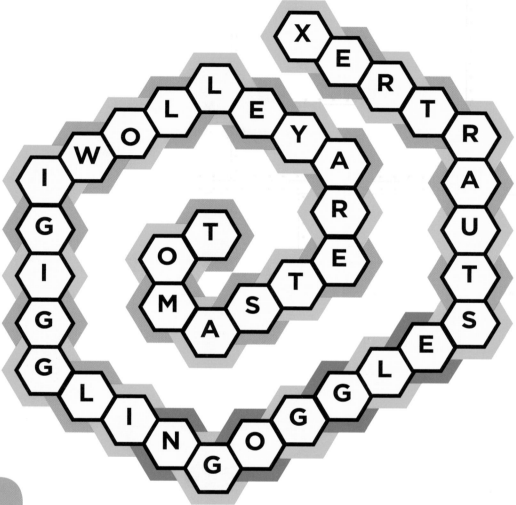

CLUES

1. The two-eyed, spiky-haired Minion who looks a little like Phil (3).

2. Every Minion needs a _ _ _ _ _ _ (6).

3. The gadget used to make things smaller is the Shrink _ _ _ (3).

4. A very Minion-y colour (6).

5. A Minion hair disguise (3).

6. What Minions spend most of their time doing (8).

7. The Minion eye covers (7).

8. The one-eyed Minion who was shaken like a glow stick (6).

9. The Minions' dinosaur master (1-3).

ANSWERS ON page 61

A LITTLE ODD

The Minions are up to something!

One of these groups is different to all the others.
Which tower of Minions is the odd one out?

a

b

c

d

e

f

ANSWERS ON page 61

Nice, Evil Minion!

Colour this Minion's hungry purple buddy.

MINION GAMES

Want to turn your friends and family into a mega Minion gang?

Try these villainous games and you'll be feeling more yellow in no time.

TALK MINIONESE

Bello! How long can you last without using any real words?
Get together with your Minion gang and try to talk like a Minion!

Use funny sounds and gibberish words while you try to hold a conversation. The first person to break and use a real word loses!

PIN THE GOGGLE ON THE MINION

Draw an extra-large version of Stuart, then colour or paint him. Now create lots of single goggle eyes by layering circles of brown, white and black paper and gluing together.

Gather some friends and take turns to be blindfolded and see who can get Stuart's eye closest to the middle!

WHO'S THE MINION MASTER?

Get your group to sit in a circle and start to slowly tap your legs then clap in a clockwork rhythm. Take turns round the circle, and every time you all clap someone has to name a character from the Minions.

As you progress, increase the rhythm and keep going until someone can't name a character on time – they're out! Keep playing until there's only one person left: the Minion Master!

SILLY STORY-MAKER

Get a clean sheet of paper and a pen.
You can play this with three people, but the more, the better.

You each take a turn to write a line of a silly Minion story. When someone's written the first line, they pass it on to the next person. That person can read the previous line, and then write their own. Before they pass it on, they should fold over the first line; only two lines should be showing at any time. Keep going round until you cover the page – then stop and read the comedy mayhem!

MINION NOUGHTS AND CROSSES

You can cut these Minions out of your book and use them as many times as you like on the grid below.
- You'll need two players, and each should pick their Minion.
- Take turns to place one Minion in the grid.
- Whoever gets three in a row first, in any direction, is the winner!

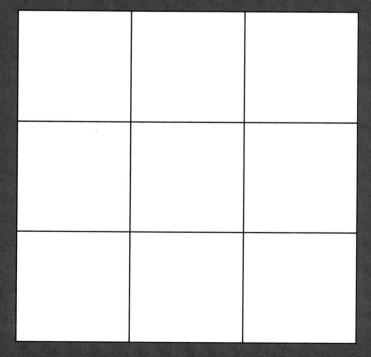

MASTERMIND QUIZ

How well do you know your favourite yellow buddies?

1 Which skateboarding Minion is this?

a Stuart

c Carl

b Jerry

2 Which Minion loves to dress up as a French maid?

a Bob

c Phil

b Tim

3 Which two Minions only have one eye?

a Tim and Tom

c Stuart and Carl

b Jerry and Stuart

4 Which Minion is a HUGE golf fan?

a Kevin

c Carl

b Dave

5 Which word is not real Minionese?

a Kampai

c Tatatu

b Poopaye

6 Who was the Minions' first ever master?

a T. Rex

c Dracula

b Caveman

7 What outfit do they wear to serve Gru?

a Military uniforms

c Dungarees and gloves

b Hats and belted trousers

8 Which Minion accidentally fires a rocket blaster?

a Kevin

c Tom

b Dave

9 Which Minion is dressed as a baby?

a Tim

c Carl

b Phil

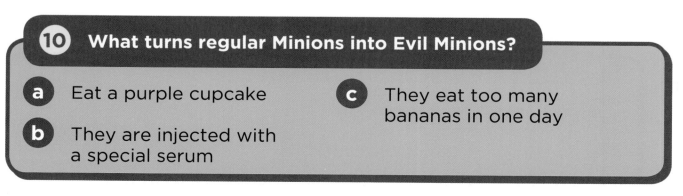

10 What turns regular Minions into Evil Minions?

a Eat a purple cupcake

c They eat too many bananas in one day

b They are injected with a special serum

MASTERMIND QUIZ

11 Which silly thing did the Minions do?

a Tricked Gru with a whoopee cushion

b Dressed Phil up as a toilet paper mummy

c Took photocopies of Jorge's bottom

12 Which two Minions like their hair nicely combed?

a Stuart and Dave

b Jerry and Tom

c Dave and Tim

13 Which Minion is scared of strange noises?

a Jerry

b Kevin

c Phil

14 Which of these weapons are real in Minion-world?

a Shrink Ray

b Cupcake blaster

c Laser goggles

15 What do Minions love most?

a Bananas, space travel and serum injections

b Bananas, lullabies and cupcakes

c Bananas, masters and bottom jokes

RESULTS

0 - 5

Banana Beginner
You'll need to hang out with the Minions a little more if you want to reach expert level. Read through this book again for a banana boost.

6 - 10

Goggle-eyed Expert
Well done! You've certainly got some expert knowledge of the little yellow guys. Just brush up a little, and you'll be a mastermind in no time.

11 - 15

Minion Mastermind
Banana-rific! You're the smartest Minion genius on the planet. Do a Minion dance to celebrate your master status.

IT'S TIME FOR
ANSWERS

PAGE 12

H	N	S	G	I	G	G	L	E	H	G	N	F	A	P	F
N	T	A	U	P	Y	O	H	D	O	L	D	E	G	N	V
G	H	O	I	S	O	G	M	G	R	E	N	I	G	S	N
Y	N	P	T	O	N	G	N	R	K	H	O	H	L	O	H
O	S	B	A	P	P	L	E	K	H	S	Y	C	E	P	N
Y	A	P	R	D	N	E	P	H	O	N	S	S	H	A	P
S	U	G	S	I	Y	S	P	O	R	Y	E	I	T	N	D
M	A	S	T	E	R	O	D	R	K	K	K	M	N	H	R
A	O	B	E	T	A	K	H	W	H	O	O	N	O	R	A
D	T	O	N	P	B	A	N	A	N	A	A	D	V	K	O
Y	A	A	K	H	U	H	A	H	S	G	R	Y	E	H	B
E	S	B	A	N	A	N	S	B	G	A	A	P	R	O	E
L	H	O	Y	S	D	A	N	C	E	K	K	R	A	R	T
L	O	T	P	N	N	A	T	O	D	T	Y	N	L	H	A
O	A	P	Y	A	O	P	D	H	S	N	O	T	L	E	K
W	E	S	I	U	G	S	I	D	O	T	A	P	S	P	S

One of the Minions' favourite gross gadgets is the fart gun.

PAGE 23

				S		
				T	I	M
				U		
		K		A		
	J	E	R	R	Y	
		V		T		
P	H	I	L			
		N		D		
	B		C	A	R	L
T	O	M		V		
	B			E		

a. Tim
b. Tom
c. Carl
d. Bob
e. Jerry
f. Stuart
g. Kevin
h. Phil
i. Dave

PAGE 24

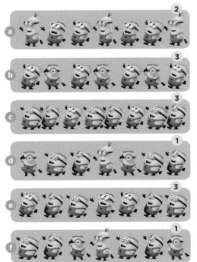

PAGE 28
1. d, **2.** c, **3.** a, **4.** e, **5.** b

PAGE 30
a 3, **b.** 5, **c.** 2, **d.** 1, **e.** 4

PAGE 32
There are 675 Minions.

PAGE 34
1. False, **2.** True, **3.** False, **4.** True, **5.** True,
6. True, **7.** False, **8.** False, **9.** False.

PAGE 35

PAGE 47

PAGE 50
1. f (Carl), **2.** h (Tim), **3.** d (Tom),
4. e (Phil), **5.** g (Bob), **6.** a (Dave),
7. c (Stuart), **8.** b (Kevin), **9.** i (Jerry).

PAGE 51
1. Tom, **2.** Master, **3.** Ray,
4. Yellow, **5.** Wig, **6.** Giggling, **7.** Goggles,
8. Stuart, **9.** T. Rex.

PAGE 52
Tower d is the odd one out. Phil
(the middle Minion) has no hair.

PAGE 56
1. a, **2.** c, **3.** b, **4.** a, **5.** c, **6.** a,
7. c, **8.** b, **9.** b, **10.** b, 11. c,
12. a, **13.** a, **14.** a, **15.** c.

**DID YOU
FIND ALL
THE HIDDEN
GOGGLES?**

The letters in the goggles spell out
DESPICABLE.